A Black

Country Chap's

Life Of Rhyme

JOHNNY 'MOGS' MORRIS

APS BOOKS
Est. Stourbridge 2014

APS Books,
The Stables Field Lane,
Aberford,
West Yorkshire,
LS25 3AE

APS Books is a subsidiary of the APS Publications imprint

www.andrewsparke.com

First published worldwide by APS Books in 2023

Black Country photographs courtesy of Black Country Museum
Cover artwork by David George
Santa illustration by Adam Morris

A catalogue record for this book is available from the British Library

www.johnnymogs.co.uk

I would like to dedicate this book to the people of the Black Country, the unique way they speak and their sheer saftness.

Introduction

If you are a poetry lover or a student of the English Language, then this pamphlet may not be for you. The poems aren't particularly 'poetic' and some of the words share only a passing resemblance to English.

This collection of dialect poems is intended to celebrate the uniqueness of the people of The Black Country, the way we speak and our sheer saftness. Hopefully some of them will give you a loff!

What is the Black Country?

Well, I think there is some disagreement as to exactly what lies within the region's borders. In general terms it is part of the West Midlands containing the metropolitan boroughs of Dudley , Sandwell, Wolverhampton and Walsall. It includes towns like Tipton, Bilston, Halesowen, Stourbridge and West Bromwich, but definitely not the city of Birmingham! For centuries the area has been at the heart of a wide range of the country's manufacturing industries. Many towns had steelworks and iron foundries, One in Netherton made the anchor for Titanic. In the late 19th century the BC was the centre of chain making for the world, while Stourbridge and the surrounding area is still renowned for its glass making.

The dialect is believed that the Black Country dialect is the closest to the Middle English spoken back in the time of Chaucer. In particular the sound of vowels were quite different and changed to the way they are pronounced today during a shift in standard English between the time of Chaucer and Shakespeare.

I am not claiming to be an expert on the subtleties of the dialect, there are just so many differences and quirks throughout the region to say what is 'normal'. I will admit up front that, although I have lived all my life in the Black Country, I do not speak with a broad accent and tend not to use many of the words in everyday conversation. However, I am surrounded by people that do

Word Definitions and phrases are included at the end of the book for anything you can't guess. poems. Although I believe that many are not unique to the Black Country and are probably used elsewhere in the English speaking world, even in the Black Country, some may be restricted to fairly small areas like a single town or even a street. Hopefully the meaning of any I have omitted will be fairly obvious.

Correct spelling is something that I cannot guarantee as there is no Oxford Black Country Dictionary, although an unofficial one produced by Steve Edwards has proved useful. Searching on the Web has just unearthed inconsistencies.

So where I'm not sure, I have spelt a word phonetically to try and give the reader   an idea of how it may be pronounced, although it does seem to vary.

For example I have heard the word floor pronounced by different people as 'flowa' to rhyme with 'shower' or 'blower' or even 'fewer'.

General 'rules' of the Black Country dialect (as I understand them):

1. As with many dialects around the country, there is a habit of dropping the leading 'h' of words and the 'g' at the end of 'ing' words. I have largely avoided the convention of replacing these missing letters with apostrophes, as there would be swarms of the blighters on every page.

2. There is a tendency to add an extra syllable to a word, such as Fower instead of four, or spoowen for spoon. Other words seem to be enlongated like 'fairce' for 'face' etc.

3. Personal pronouns tend to get swapped around, so that (h)er is used instead of she, we instead of us and us instead of our.

4. I tends to get pronounced as 'Ar', but as this is also the word used for 'yes' I have left it as an 'I' in the poems to try and avoid confusion.

5. As for vowels, as mentioned earlier, these tend not to be pronounced as they are in standard English. So the 'a' sound becomes an 'o' sound as in stond for the word 'stand'. The 'o' becomes a 'u' as in 'lung' for 'long'.The 'ou' sound in the word 'out' gets elongated as 'aaht', and so on.

6. As with all 'rules' of the English Language, there are many exceptions. Like the 'I before   except after ce' rule, which doesn't always apply.

All I can say is the Black Country dialect is as different as any other in the British Isles and is prone to all of the inconsistencies of the Mother Tongue.

I have recorded some of the poems and put them on my SoundCloud page. The QR Codes are included at the end of the book if you would like to hear my version of the dialect. Otherwise please just read the poems and have a lof.

Foreword

Many years ago I started a journey to find out who i really was. At the time a lot of my academic work moved in tandem. I was at a sort of crossroads where my own voice was battling to get out over the voice i had acquired over the years of trying to 'fit in' somewhere. This journey has been such a joy not only in unearthing my own and others stories and experiences but also in finding a realisation that every utterance we make is part of who we are. That utterance not only connects us to our past but also determines our future. How we see the world, how we make decisions. One step on the journey opens endless doors in being me/ us.

Our language (that of the Black Country) is full of raw eloquence, vitality a rhythm that beats of its industrial heritage. Committing our words to paper is not only the most exciting process, it also becomes a bespoke process where our own histories determine what others will see. A term used in my field of practise is 'eye' dialect. This is what is seen in the writers head and this(particularly here in the Black Country with so many varieties can vary from town to town. How a Tipp'n Mon sees a word will be very different to someone in Black'y'eeth. This for me makes reading dialect works all the more challenging because the reader has to get inside the writer's history then use their own 'eye dialect to covert and live the work. In my own writings I advise people to wait until they have found the pulse of each piece and then read the piece out loud. Hear the wonderful intonations of our words , our history, that which has shaped us.

Moggsy's new volume of work is all that i expect. bally loffable, touchin', tender, and a wonderful struggle to discover his voice then belt it out loud in my own. As an exercise I gave some of John's work to Keith (Yorkshire Mon) and Tom (Brummie) to read out on the Omma (Radio show). Without the native inherent feel for Black Countryness their valiant attempts illustrated how (as with all regional languages) it has to come from inside. The voice is part of the very core of who we are. I'm not going to single any piece out . All I advise readers to do is drown yourself in the stories, characters, embedded rhythms. When you read it , stand up and read it loud. This is a triumph in voice, place, identity and it makes me very proud to be a Black Country Mon.

Billy Spakemon (aka Dr Brian Dakin)
Visiting Research Fellow
Aston University

Contents

and flows into the River Severn in Worcestershire, and so is known as The Severn Stour by the Rivers Authority. It has played a huge part in the area's industrial history. Supporting the manufacture of Stourbridge's famous glassware, the many steelworks and iron forges, some of which date back to the Middle Ages, as well as other industries outside the Black Country like Kidderminster's carpets.

Word Definitions ~ 40

A Black Country
Chap's Life Of Rhyme

Why's It Called The Black Country?

Some say the Black Country woz gid its name
By Queen Vicky one day on a visit,
Er gawked from er train and said, "Hey Bert,
Tay very claine up ere, is it!"

"Look at them chimbleys belchin' out smoke
From fac'tries caked in sooty shite."
Though yow'da thought er'd not put it like that,
Queens am posh and usually polite.

"Ev'rything's black," er said, "Even the sky,
It looks a right shit-owul of a plairce,
Them folks am common and covered in crap,
Doe think they've ever ad soap on their fairce."

"Tell the train driver we doe wanna stay,"
It's so cack here one doe wish to look,
We ay sid such a black country afower."
And it's said, from that day, the name stuck.

With that er woz off, winda blinds shut
As er train chuffed off daahn the track,
Er only trip to that part of er realm,
Er said, "Yow woe catch we comin' back!"

But what er day twig, as er eaded wum,
Woz that Black Country folk never tire,
They'd slog day 'n' night to mek the whales turn,
And help pay for er massive empire.

Them fact'ries woz the eart of the nation,
Most stuff yow could buy then, woz med there,
The folks day mind bein covered in shite

1

And breathin the crap in the air.

But if er cum back up this way today
Er oodn't arf get a surprise,
Coz a cent'ry after er med that trip
Er'd be shocked at the Black Country's demise.

The chimbleys am gone, the whales turn no
moower,
And the eart of a nation's stone jed,
Where fact'ries once stood mekin stuff for the
world,
They've now built shappin centres instead.

A Black Country Chap

I'm a Black Country chap,
So doe gimme no crap
'Bout me soundin like some kinda Brummy.
Coz them people from Brum,
Am as common as they come,
And when they spake, they doe arf spake funny.

If I come from Newcastle,
Yow'd not gimme no assle,
And say I sounded like some kinda Jock.
If from Hereford I came,
I'm sure yow'd refrain,
From sayin, "Warro Taff, where's yer flock?"

And if by some chance
I come from French France,
'Ud yow say, "Bonjuwer, est vous Belgique?"
And if I woz Dutch,
I'd not thank yow too much,
If yow said I woz German - damned cheek!

Yow'd not get no thanks
Callin Canadians, Yanks,
It's just summat of which they'm quite fussy.
And Portuguese in the main,
They doe come from Spain,
And a New Zealand bloke bay an Aussie.

Now doe get me wrung,
Coz when all's said and done,
I'm sure that Brummies am really nice folk,
But me identity,
Is precious to me,

And I just ay a Brummagem bloke.

I'm no racontuwer,
No delusions of granduwer,
I bay posh, not me, nah, far from it.
I come from Halesowen,
And I've writ this ere poem,
To say, I'm a Black Country chap, and proud onnit.

Ave Yow Sid 'Ow Big The Sun Is?

"Ave yow sid ow big the sun is?"
Me mairte sez when Ar sid 'im today,
I sez, "It doe look that big to me."
E sez, "Daft sod, it's miles away."

"Ave yow felt ow ot the sun is?"
E sez, "Meks me sweat like a pig.
And yet it's stuck miles aaht in spairce.
To be that ot, it must be big."

"Ave yow sid ow bright the sun is?"
E sez, "Ar, it's moower than a glimmer."
I sez, "T'urts me eyes when Ar look,
I'll tek a peek tonight when it's dimmer."

"Ave yow sid ow big the sun is?"
E sez, "It's bigger than yow'da guessed,
But yow cor tell stood aaht in yower fode,
Yow needs to get close to see best."

"Ave yow sid ow big the sun is?
Well, if yow wanna see it proper,"
E sez, "Yow need to goo way aaht in spairce,
Then yow'll see, it's a bloody whopper."

Well, ave *yow* sid ow big the sun is?
I doe care what me ode mairte says,
It cor be that big, coz in the Black Country
Sometimes yow doe see it for days.

Er's Gooin' Saft

I think er's gooen saft yer know,
Thought p'raps one day er might,
Sometimes er bay on this planet,
The poor ooman just ay right.

Er just keeps on misplaircin things,
And I bay one to mek a fuss,
But er faculties am fairdin
And I think er's gettin wuss.

We woz gooen aaht this mornin
Er sez, "Where's me ganzy gone?"
I watched er search for yonks then sez,
"Yow've got the damned thing on!"

Then er cor find er car kays,
Er sez, "I just doe understond,
I've sid 'em somewhere, I'm sure I ave."
I sez, "They'm in yer bloody ond!"

Er fun er ondbag in the oven,
And er pus tucked up in bed,
Then er glasses, they goo missin;
I fun 'em, stuck on er yead.

By the time we gets to Asda
I really cor tek any moower,
Then to cap it all er turns and sez,
"What ave we come in ere fower?"

Ar, I think er's gooen yampy,
Er's gooen saft, it's plairn to see,
Still, I s'pose it ay surprisin coz
The poor wench is married to me!

6

Aaht In The Street

Most wikends and school olidees
we'd be aaht early, in the street,
catlicked fizzogs, hair frowsty,
breffus stains still damp on ganzies.

Curb stones for goalposts,
we'd lamp the bladder around,
trample gardens to fetch wayward shots,
skraze knees on the tarmac pitch,
and mek the occasional car wait
for franzied kids to get out the oss road.

Other times, we'd get bikes aaht, or tramwagst,
urtle daahn racetrack pavements
scatterin folk in all directions;
come winter sometimes, it might be sledges.

We'd goo scrumpin',
ait opples 'til we got bally airk,
stick what woz left in the rowad
and cheer like clarnets
as they got craunched by a passing truck or sharra.

We'd goo clartin' abaaht
daahn the cut,
or clomberin trees
on the bonk by the brook,

we'd light a fire,
mek flirters and tek potshots at the spuggies,
 chuck bibbles at windas of an empty fact'ry,
sit round choblin suck

or maybe try a fake one of we'd nicked off us moms.

We'd stay aaht all day,
even when it got black over the back of Bill's Mother's,
Rairce wum when we woz clammed to jeath,
sometimes soaked,
wommuck us tay down
and be aaht agen 'til called in for bed.

We wor bad kids, just the way it woz back then.
There wor no i-phones or 'puters,
wor fussed 'baaht watchin tele.
We day mooch about the ouse mytherin us moms,
we woz aaht in the street
or daahn the brook,
avin a loff, mekin us own fun.

Doe Come Daahn Ere

Yow doe wanna come daahn ere mairte,
Coz it ay a sairfe plairce to be,
There's danger, lurks in the shadders,
Just look what appened to me.

Nah, yow doe wanna come daahn ere mairte,
Tho' at fust glance it may look nice,
But afower yow as a look around,
If I woz yow mairte, Ar'd think twice.

Coz it's really quite unpleasant ere,
It's a plairce yow'm gonna ate,
It's damp, there's cobwebs everywhere
That yow cor see 'til it's too late.

Nah, tay as nice as yow might think,
I've fun that out for meself,
Coz nosin round this dingey plairce
Just ay no good for yer ealth.

So yow doe wanna come daahn ere,
With that carefree attitude,
Coz yow'll end up, ung up like me
On a web, as spider food.

The Night Aer Kid Let Loose

Oh, the night aer Kid let loose.
E day arf tek some abuse,
Even ad it on the local news,
The night aer Kid let loose.

E'd bin on a curried spraaht diet,
'Is bally, e said, woz a riot,
It shattered the peace and quiet,
The night aer Kid let loose.

Well, aer Kid woz broken earted,
That day 'is wench and 'im ad parted,
Couldn't stop once e ad started,
The night aer Kid let loose.

E started late in the afternoon,
Continued by the light of the moon,
E played a lung and soulful tune,
The night aer Kid let loose.

Said e'd bin moved deep daahn inside,
Then e leaned back and smiled with pride,
Smelt like summat ad bloody died,
The night aer Kid let loose.

Mother said er'd ad er daahbts,
When gidin him them curried spraahts,
Aer Kid said, "Ooh, it's better aaht,"
The night aer Kid let loose.

There woz summat in the air that night,
The neighbours dared not strike a light,
They said, "That boy's guts, cor be right!"
The night aer Kid let loose.

Day arf tek Dudley by surprise,
It attracted great swarms of flies,
It brung tears to yer bloody eyes,
The night aer Kid let loose.

As it wafted through Dudley town,
People fainted for miles around,
Streets echoed with that dreadful sound,
The night aer Kid let loose.

"It day appen," some tried to pretend,
But it's now a Black Country legend,
When Dudley woz gassed and deafened,
The night aer Kid let loose.

Bein A Black Country Mon

I drink bootloods o' beer and lager
And ait scratchings by the ton,
I doe goo wum until I cor stond
Coz I'm a Black Country mon.

The bookies as most o' me ackers,
I doe let er know what I'm spendin,
I stays in the pub 'til er's asleep,
So's I ducks another ear bendin'.

I always goz aaht with no coot on,
Ar, even in the ice and the snow,
Er sez, "Yow'm saft, doe yow feel the cowed?!"
Well, bein a Black Country mon, yer doe.

I 'as fights, most nights, when I'm bletted ,
When I spake, I swear and Ar cuss,
I do try to keep out the oss road
Coz, it's what a Black Country mon does.

But me mairtes say that someat ay right,
The Black Country cor be where Ar'm from,
Coz yow cor goo round spoutin poems,
And be a proper Black Country mon.

Cor Cook

Er meks me dinner and tay,
But I really wish er day,
Coz the poor wench just cor cook to save er bloody
life.
Er faggots am always raw,
Er burgers bost yer jaw,
And tryin to cut er gravy bends yer bloody knife.

Er frozen chips am a riddle,
Burnt, and froze in the middle.
Er choux pastry is like chewin a piece of leather.
Er taters turn to mush,
Er stew teks a double flush,
And er groaty dick clogs the plumbin all together.

Well, er cor mek scones or cairks,
And I've sid er burn corndlairks,
Er struggles to mek a cheese and pickle sandwich.
I've bought er cook'ry books,
Tries to read 'em when er cooks,
And sez, "Ave these things bin writ in a foreign
language?"

I doe get a Sundee roastt,
Er mainly does me toast,
I doe get much of that, once the burnt bits am cut
off.
If I goz off daahn the pub,
And er sez, "I've done some grub.
Am yow aitin fust or what?" Well, I just loff.

Ev'ry day the ooman toils,

Er microwaves and boils,
It's amazin, ow er can kill off any flavour.
When I refuse a plairteful,
Er sez, that I'm ungrairteful,
but er fittle just 'ay some'at a bloke can savour.

Well I think er's 'ad enough,
Er's gone off in an 'uff,
I'm left alone to read through er cook'ry books.
I tried to cook me tay.
But then fetched a tek-away,
Yow know, this cookin lark bay as easy as it looks.

We Woz Brung Up Proper

We woz brung up proper, we woz,
Day ave no airs 'n' grairces,
We woz poower, just did 'n' med do,
Always ad dirt on us fairces.

We woz learnt to 'ave good manners,
Gotta lampin if we woz rude,
We day spake with food in us gobs
Coz it wor often we 'ad food.

The bog woz aaht in the garden,
Doin yer ablutions we'd ate,
Coz when yow went in the winter
Yer arse ood get froze to the sate.

Them kids today doe know they'm born
We ad it tough back in my day.
There wor no teles or computers
And we still turned out ok.

Day ave things we couldn't pay fower,
Ya wanted cash; ya gotta job,
Yow day sit round with yer donny out
Like some benefit scroungin slob.

We day goo blamin immigrants,
For the things we adn't got
We day expect nothin for nowt,
We woz appy with our lot.

We day mooch about at wum all day,
Day Facebook, text or Twitter,
We'd goo aaht and mek us own fun,
Even when aaht, it woz bitter.

Mum worked day 'n' night, ad six kids
But still that udn't stop er,
Er learnt we all right from wrong,
Ar, coz we woz brung up proper.

Bloke On An Oss

There once woz a bloke on an oss,
Reached a river e wanted to cross,
The oss said, "Gerra boat,
'Coz osses doe float,
In a boat, I can row us across."

Tramwags

Shooda sid us kids on tramwags,
Bombin daahn the ill,
Feet up, onds off breks,
Squailin at the thrill.
Avin a bostin time,
Gooen where we please,
Bashin yeads and elbas,
Tekin skin off onds and knees.
We'd goo crashin into lompposts,
Knock ode women off their feet,
Yow cud ear the whales a rumblin
As we urtled daahn the street.
We'd dodge the occasional car,
Drag us feet when slowin daahn,
We'd splash through ev'ry puddle
And avoid things warm 'n' braahn.
We'd goo aaht in any weather,
We'd fly off any crest,
Woz appy times we ad back then,
Them tramwag days woz best.

Er's Me Ooman

Er's me ooman ay er.
Er's me bird, ar, me bit of stuff,
The only wench, day run a mile
When er sid me in the buff.

Er's me ooman ay er.
Ar, what ar calls 'Me Ode Trout',
If some bloke tried chattin er up
I'd sort the begger aaht.

Er's me ooman ay er.
I giz er chocies and flowers,
I listens while er witters on
And doe tek a breath for hours.

Er's me ooman ay er.
So, I puts up with all the naggin,
Er moans and groans and bends me ear,
Er tongue is always waggin.

Er's me ooman ay er.
Er may belch and swear and fart,
But er'll always be me ooman,
Ar, that wench as stole me eart!

A Black Country Spider

Just bog off! Doe yow cum round ere
And goo bostin all me stuff,
I've bin and spun aaht all me webs,
And it's took me lung enough.

So doe yow cum clodhopping round,
Cor yow tek a bit mower care!
Coz the plairces yow'm a trapesin,
I've got me webs all strung out there?

I've put 'em there for a reason,
Tay to wrap round yower saft fairce,
I'm tryin to catch meself some tay,
Coz fittle daahn ere is scarce.

They really ay that ard to see,
Try openin yer bloody eyes,
I doe wanna catch some fat-arsed bloke,
All I want's a few juicy flies.

Now what's that thing there in yower ond,
That meks that weird suckin noise?
Coz every web yow point it at
That funny suckin thing destroys.

Now all me webs ave disappeared,
Well to me that's bloody theft.
Yow've ad ev'ry one I've ever med,
Yow've ad the lot, there bay one left.

Why cor yow leave me stuff aloon,
I doe come round and nick all yowers,
I'll ave to mek 'em all agen,
It's gonna tek me bloody hours.

Them webs woz where I use to live!
But yow doe care what yow ave done,
Yow and that funny suckin thing
Ave clained me out of ouse and wum.

Cor Fly

I sez, "I'm just a babby bird."
I doe think me mother eard,
As er stared into the distance, a tear in er eye.
Er sez, "Son, I've done me best,
But it's time yow flew the nest."
I sez, "I cor do that, coz i cor bloody fly."

Er sez, "Doe gimme that crap,
Yow'm a fully feathered chap,
And ow'm yer gonna know, 'til yow've gid it a try?
I'm afraird the time as come,
It's time yow woz leavin wum."
I sez, "Doe mek me do it Mum; I cor bloody fly."

"It's the easiest of things,"
Er sez, "Just stick aaht yer wings,
Then stond there on that branch and leap into the
sky.
Goo on, get them wings unfurled,
Yow gerroff and see the world."
I sez, "I'm gooen nowhere, coz I cor bloody fly."

Well to show er mother's love,
Er gid me a bloody shove,
And fightin back the tears er sez, "I loves yow son,
goodbye."
As I plummet to the graahnd,
From er tree me mum looks daahn,
And sez, "Well, who'd a thought it? Yow cor
bloody fly!"

Bob On 'Er

Er ay arf got a bob on er,
Thinks er's posher than all of us,
Er woe goo shappin in Asda
Or goo plairces on the buz.

Er doe arf look daahn er snidge at folk,
Ar know with me, er bay impressed,
When I aits me tay off a tray and
Watch tele in pants and vest.

Er doe goo nowhere in er curlers,
Sounds like the queen when er spakes,
Doe sup er tay aahta saucers,
As a fork when aitin cairkes.

Doe arf think a lot of erself
Buys er drawers from M&S,
Doe belch, or fart, or pick 'er snidge
Well, at least that's what er sez.

Sez er lean-to's a conservatory,
It's a patio, it bay a fode,
Tay the cut er lives by, and sez
Er doe goo in the oss rowad.

Er ay arf got a bob on er,
Thinks er's posher than Judy Dench,
Er seems to forget, under it all,
Er's still a Black Country wench.

Attic

Loffed? I'm in the attic.
Er knows that I'm asthmatic
And all the dust up ere's gonna mek me wheeze
and sneeze.
But er doe bloody care,
Sez. "It's in the loft somewhere,
I needs it now so, woe yer just goo and get it
please."

Loffed? I'm in the attic,
Amazed ow high we stack it,
All the piles of stuff I ay sid for many years.
We doe throw now't away,
Coz we might need it one day.
So it gets chucked up ere and then quickly
disappears.

Loft? I really cooda cried,
As I crawl around inside,
Er sez, "It's there somewhere." But me, I've got me
daahbts.
Cor think last time I sin it.
Er sez, "Well , I day bin it,"
As er waits for me to pass it, with er donnies aaht.

Loffed? I'm in the attic,
"It's there," er's still emphatic,
I sez, "I cor find it! Come up, maybe you can.
Yow could search a wik or moower
Not find what yow'm lookin fower,
I bet somewhere up ere is Shergar and Lord Lucan!

Loffed? I'm in the attic,

Tryin to be acrobatic,
Me foot's gone through the sailin, I may ave urt
meself.
Loft? I'm bloody ecstatic!
Er shouts, "It wor in the attic,
Yow can come down now, I've fun it ere on the
shelf."

Doe Babbies Grizzle?

Oh doe them babbies grizzle?
Ar, doe they whinge and blart?
And yow cor bloody stop 'em
Once the blighters start.

Seems they'm always wantin summat
But just what, that's the riddle.
Am they ungry? Am they thirsty?
Pants full of babby piddle?

They'm always bloody moanin,
The sods ain't never appy,
But tay them what mops their puke up
And siz the contents of their nappy.

I've ad enough of wipin arses,
All I want's a bit of peace,
Coz even when I'm tryin to sleep
The babby grizzlin just doe cease.

They woe tell yer why they'm grizzling,
Doe they just get on yer tits!
Night and day they just keep squailin
They am noisy little shits.

They just lie there in a paddy
Demandin moower 'n' mower,
Sometimes I bloody wonder
What dun we ave babbies fower?

Now I doe ate babbies as such,
Without 'em mankind ud fizzle,
But sometimes I wish they day exist
Coz doe them babbies grizzle!

Nan's

Back when I woz a kid
we'd goo round Nan's of a Sundee.
Mom ood mek me stick me best clobber on
like we woz gooen somewhere posh.

We'd ait us lunch round the tairble,
me getting towud off
for rilin about
or slummockin' in me sate.

When no one wor looking
I'd slip sprouts off me fork, feed 'em the wammel
and still be odgin cowud veg round me plairt when
they woz all done.
"Get it down ya wazzin lover," Nan 'ud say,
"Yow'll 'ave it dark else!"

After, I'd avve to sit there for yonks
while the grow'd-ups canted round the fire.
Nan gooen on abaaht 'that Christmas the cut froze',
or 'the night they bombed Tipp'n',
or 'what it woz like when er woz lickle
and they day never ave no fittle'.

When I woz ode enough
Nan 'ud let me chuck coal on the fire,
lung as I minded er tranklements on the mantle.
"Mind 'em," er'd say, "they'm full of memories.
Doe want some great lummock bostin none."

When er got really ode, Nan ad to ave an ooman
round to modge for er,
to do the washin and clainin and such,

coz er couldn't manage no moower;
and er'd come round owern for lunch.

These days, doe see er much.
When I dun, it bay er, if yer know what I mean.
Er just gawks at we,
Like weem strairngers.

Dad got rid of Nan's tranklements
when er ad to move.
There wor no mantle to stick 'em on,
nor a fire to sit round cantin.
Not that er spakes much any moower.

Er stories am gone now;
wish I'd listened, back then
round Nan's.

Lazy Eye

When I woz young the optician said
That I'd got a lazy eye.
Me mom said er day understond,
And then er began to cry.

E said, "Now it tay a problem,
There's just one eye that's got poor sight,
But there's summat what I can do
That'll maybe put it right."

"I'll put a patch over 'is good eye,
And that'll mek the bad 'un weark."
When I eard what e'd said, I thought,
This optician bloke's a berk.

To goo and cover up the good eye
To me just sounded crazy,
Coz all that that woz gonna do
Woz mek *that* buggar lazy.

So I sez, "Now listen me mucka,
Dun yow know what yow'm a-doin?
If I cor look aaht me good eye,
Ow'll I see where I'm a gooen?"

"And ow do I play me footee
With me good eye covered up?
I've gotta big gairme this wikend,
It's the fust round o' the cup."

"Well, I cor turn up on Satdee
With me eye beneath a patch,
I needs to see what I'm a-doin,
It's a very important match."

"So yow con stick yer pirate's eye-patch,
Coz I just bay gonna wear it."
But me mom said, "It's for yer own good,
Yow'll just ave to grin and bear it."
So, I wore the patch and plaired the gairme,
But I wor no use at all,
Coz yow cor play cowin footee,
With only one eye on the ball.

It day goo well, we woz six nil daahn
With only twenty minutes gone,
When another went in, I thought to meself,
I cor see us winning this one!"

The fust arf dragged, I day enjoy it,
It really did goo slowly.
Then at arf-time the manager sez,
"Yow ay a patch on our ode goalie."

"We ay got a sub, but yow'm comin off,
Ar, I'd rather play with ten.
Yow may as well sell them footie boots,
Coz yow woe be playin agen."

I went back to that optician bloke,
Said, "I'll gid yower patch a miss."
And I ay bin back to see 'im,
Not from that day through to this.

So me lazy eye's still lazy,
Me mother sez er thinks it's spread,
Coz for 30 odd year, I ay ad a job
And some days, I doe get aahta bed.

Domestic Bliss

Er doe let me do a tap at wum
Sez I really cor be trusted,
Coz everythin I try and do
I cock-up, or stuff gets busted.
Er woe let me do the ironin,
Sez, I doe get the creases aaht,
Er woe let me do the dustin,
Coz I just move the dust abaaht.

Er woe let me touch the vacuum
Coz I cor control the suckin,
Er woe let me mek the dinner
Coz I'm bloody crap at cookin.
Woe even let me claine the crocks,
I always bost a cup or plairte,
Decoratin, er sez that's aaht,
Coz I cor ang pairper strairght.

The washin machine, I cor use that,
Coz I put colours in with whites,
I bay allowed to mek the bed,
Er sez I just doe do it right.
Woe even let me tidy up
I put stuff in the wrung plairce
But I leave me pants chucked on the flowa
And doe er play er bloody fairce.

Er woe let me mow the lawn coz
The grassbox fills with petals,
And er woe let me do the weedin,
I cor tell flowers from nettles,
Woe let me pairnt the garden fence,

I trample on the bedding plants.
Woe let me ang the washin aaht,
I let the neighbours see er pants.

Woe let me do no DIY
Er sez I'm lackin any skill,
Er's idden all me tools and took
The plug off me 'lectric drill.
Woe even let me wash the car
Coz, er sez I scratch the pairnt,
Er sez to leave it all aloon
Coz an andymon I ain't.

Er woe let me do a bloody thing,
So now I doe even try,
There's now't I do is any good
I think er standards am too high.
So, we ave an understondin
And it all boils down to this -
I sit on me arse, er does it all,
And so we get domestic bliss.

I Think Santa's
A Black Country Chap

I think Santa might be a Black Country chap,
Wears big hobnail boots and a saft floppy cap,
When 'e gets 'um from work e's covered in crap,
So, I think Santa's a Black Country chap.

Goz clomberin dahn chimblys with a big heavy sack,
Drinks boot'loods of sherry and struggles to climb back,
When at last 'e crawls out yow can see 'is bum-crack,
I think Santa's a Black Country chap.

'E doe 'arf like 'is booze, that chap Santa Clause,
And doe give a toss 'bout them 'drink flying laws',
Goz in folks' 'ouses, cor be arsed to use doors
I think Santa's a Black Country chap.

'E always seems jolly, like a Black Country bloke,
Yow always 'ear 'im loffin like 'e's just heard a joke,
Doe work in a foundry, but still stinks of smoke,
I think Santa's a Black Country chap.

'E's got a huge bally, doe do exercise,
It's easy to spot who scoffed all of the pies,
'E doe walk anywhere, the lazy git flies,
Ar, I think Santa's a Black Country chap.

'E's boon idle, all year 'e woe do a tap,
But come Christmas Eve 'e gets in a right flap,

Coz there's still loads of pressies to buy and then wrap,
I think Santa's a Black Country chap.

So, he'll rush out in a panic, but woe shap around,
Just goz in that plairce where it all costs a pound,
'Is vehicle's knackered, meks a strange jingling sound,
I think Santa's a Black Country chap.

E 'ates Christmas Day, coz they 'ave the wife's mum,
'E's glad when it's over and er's buggered off 'um,
Then all year, the lazy git woe shift of his bum,
Ar, I think Santa's a Black Country chap.

The Queen Ay Arf Posh

The Queen, er ay arf posh, Yer know,
Er ay common like any o' yow,
And though er mairtes am posh 'n' all
To er they curtsy and bow.

The crusts am cut off er sarnies.
Drinks tay from bone china cups,
Doe slurp it out of a saucer,
Er finger sticks out as er sups.

Er doe goo shappin daahn Asda,
Waitrose is the plairce that er guz,
Phil teks er daahn in 'is Rolla,
E woe let er goo on the buz.

Er doe ave a tray on er lap
Watchin TV as er aits,
Er as er tay at the tairble,
And aits it off silver plairtes.

Er ay got an outside lavvy,
Er throne room is lovely and warm.
There ay ode cars dumped on er drive,
The wammels doe crap on er lawn.

Er doe dry er smalls in the garden,
Doe fart when er's in the tub,
Er doe stop for a donor kebab
When on er way wum from the pub.

Er doe get kaylied in Marbella,
As olidays in posh plairces.
Er really likes bettin on osses
And wearin posh ats at the rairces.

Er doe slob abaaht in ode clothes,
Er always looks regal and serene,
Er doe 'F and blind', er spakes right posh,
S'pose that's why they med er The Queen.

Er doe get complairnts from the neighbours,
Let er kids play aaht in the streets,
Er may be posh, but er bay stuck up,
Er's nice to the folk that er meets.

Ar, The Queen ay arf posh yer know,
Got ouses yow could get lost in,
But er's daahn to earth, and very nice,
I think The Queen's bloody bostin!

The Severn Stour

A child of Worcestershire,
forged in the Clent Hills.
Finds its way to The Black Country,
then dips a languid toe in Staffordshire,
before easing its way to Stourport
to be consumed by the Severn.

Once, industry plotted every meander
of its short journey.
Stalked each twist and turn
as It pushed past mills,
cooled glowing glass,
and weaved a path through carpet factories.
Iron forges greedily drank in its purity
and spat out their vileness
to drown the fish in tainted water.

It gave its very soul
to the ceaseless demands,
gave its lifeblood
to feed the leaching canals
that shepherd its bewildering progress.

For centuries it was abused,
bullied from nature's intended path,
forced through culverts,
pushed under roads and buildings.

The parasitic factories and forges may be gone,
but still it struggles to catch its breath,
suffocated by a cocktail of casually discarded
poisons.

The Stour,
no Amazon or Nile,
but in its own way just as mighty.
Carried the burden on timid shoulders for so long.
It suckles on Clent's tributaries
and hides in plain sight,
as it tiptoes, unnoticed,
through the Black Country's backyard.

Word Definitions

Aaht – out.
Ackers – money.
Aer Kid – (our kid) brother or sister (usually younger).
Afower – before
Airk – ache.
Ait - eat
Ar - yes
Ay – isn't

Babby - baby
Bally – belly or stomach
Bay – not.
Bibble – small stones or pebbles.
Bin - been
Blether – talk nonsense or incessantly.
Bletted - drunk
Bladder – football or balloon.
Blart – cry.
Bonk – bank.
Bootloods a large amount (ie. Boatloads.)
Bost – break or broken
Bostin – something that's bostin is brilliant.
Braahn – brown.
Breffus - breakfast
Brummagem - Birmingham
Buz - bus

Cant – talk or gossip.
Catlick – hasty wash.

Chimbly – chimney
choblin – eating loudly.
Claine - clean
Clainin the crocks ' washing-up.
Clarnet – idiot orr fool.
Clartin about – messing around.
Clemmed – hungry.
Clemmed to jeath – REALLY hungry.
Clobber – clothes or to hit.
Clomber – climb.
Coot - coat
Cor – can't
Coz – because
Craunch – crunch.
Cut – canal

Daahbt – doubt.
Daahn – down.
Day – didn't
Doe – don't
Donnies - hands

Fake – cigarette.
Fittle - food
Fizzog – face.
Flirter – catapult usually nade with rubber bands.
Fode – backyard
Franzy – irritable, particularly fretfull children.
Frowtsy – dishevelled.
Fust – firstf

Gawk - look

Ganzy – jumper or cardigan
Gerra – get a
Gid – give, given or gave
Gleed – a cinder.
Goo - go
Gooen – going.
Goz or guz - goes
Groaty Dick – (pronounced Grawty Dick)
traditional stew like dish.

Jead - dead

Kay - key
Kaylied – drunk.

Lamp – hit.
Lampin – a thrashing or beating
Lickle – little.
Loff - laugh
Loffed - laughed
Lummock – clumsy person.

Mairte – mate (friend).
Mate – meat.
Mek - make
Modge – to fuss about doing stuff (like
housework).
Mooch – idle about bored.
Mower – more.
Myther – irritate or bother.

Odge – push about.

Ond - hand
Ooman - woman
Opple – apple.
Oss – horse.
Owern – ours.

Pus - purse

Rilin – fidgeting.

Saft – silly, stupid etc.
Sailin – ceiling
Sate - seat
Scrumpin – stealing fruit , usually apples.
Ssez - says
Sharra – coach.
Sid or sin - seen
Skraze – graze or scratch.
Slummockin – slouching
Spake - speak
Spuggies – birds, usually sparrows.
Suck – sweets.
Summat – something.

Tay – tea or isn't
Tek - take
Tramwag – kart made from wood and pram wheels.
As far as I know, a word that is only used in my
home town of Halesowen.
Tranklements – nik-naks ornaments etc.
Trapesin – walking aimlessly about
Tipp'n – Tipton, a town in the BC.

Ud – Would,

Wannel – mongrel dog
Warro - hello
Wazzin ' throat or gullet
Weem – we are.
Wench – girl
Whale - wheel
Wik - week
Woe – won't
Wommuck – to eat fast.
Wor – wasn't
Woz – was
Wum or 'um - home
Wuss - worse

Yampy – barmy, daft or losing the plot
Yead - head
Yow – you
Yowda – you would have.
Yowers – yours.
Yowm – you are.

Phrases

It's getting black over the back of Bill's Mother's
Looks like rain's on the way. From what I
understand, this may be a very old saying and not
exclusive to the Black Country, as the 'Bill' in
question is William Shakespeare.
Bob on 'er – delusions of grandeur

Keep out of the oss road – take care or get out of the way.
Yow'll ave it dark – you're taking too long.

SoundCloud Links
www.soundcloud.com/johnny-mogs/

Why's It Called The Black Country?

A Black Country Chap

Ave Yow Sin Ow Big The Sun Is

Er's Gooen Saft

Aaht In The Street

Cor Cook

Tramwags

I Cor Fly

Nan's

The Severn Stour

This is a recording that was played on the World At One program on Radio 4 in July 2020. The 'sound effects' were recorded by my wife, Sue Morris and subsequently edited into the poem by a BBC engineer.

Acknowledgements

I would like to thank everybody who has made this book possible, primarily the people of The Black Country for – well, just being Black Country folk.

Many thanks to Tim Hamilton at The Black Country Living Museum for his hard work in finding and providing the photographs.

Thanks to David George for the cover illustration and my son Adam Morris for the Santa illustration.

The Black Country Dictionary published by Steve Edwards has proved invaluable, so thanks to him for that.

I am grateful to Andrew Sparke at APS Books for picking this collection to publish, and of course thanks to you 'the reader' for reading the book.

VERSE FROM APS PUBLICATIONS
(www.andrewsparke.com)

A Black Country Chap's Life Of Rhyme (Johnny 'Mogs' Morris)
Artists 4 Syria (Various)
Backing Into The Limelight (Pete Crump)
Broken English (Andrew Sparke)
Close But Not Close Enough (Lee Benson)
Cobwebs In The Hedgerow (Wanda Pierpoint)
Drinkers Thinkers Outright Stinkers (Mark Skirving)
Dub Truth (Kokumo Noxid)
Edging Out Of The Shadows (Pete Crump)
Every Picture Hides A Friend (Lee Benson)
Failing To Be Serious (Lee Benson)
Fluid Edges (David Hamilton)
Fractured Time (Andrew Sparke)
From Bearwood And Beyond (Keith Bracey)
Goddess Woman Butterfly Human (SC Lourie)
Got It Right (Lee Benson)
Gutter Verse & The Baboon Concerto (Andrew Sparke)
I've Landed (Empress P)
Inside Looking Out (Milton Godfrey)
Irrational Thoughts Random Rhymes (HR Beasley)
Jottings and Scribbles (Lee Benson)
Just Pieces Of A Man (Kokumo Noxid)
Love & Levity (Andrew Sparke)
Meandering With Intent (Lee Benson)
Phantom Verses (Angela Patmore)
Pipe Dream (Kokumo Noxid)
Random Word Trips (Lee Benson)
Reading Rites Writing Wrongs (Ian Meacheam)
Refracted Light (Andrew Sparke)
Riding The Top Deck (John Wright)
Scratch The Sky (Lee Benson)
Shining Light Dark Matters (Ian Meacheam)

Silent Melodies (Andrew Sparke)
Silent Songs Of Owen Parsnip (Angela Patmore)
Still But Still Moving (Phil Thomson)
Stone People Glass Houses (Ian Meacheam)
Tea Among Kiwis (Andrew Sparke)
Tea and Symphony (Andrew Sparke)
Tequila & Me (Andrew Sparke)
The Boys Of Winter (Angela Patmore)
The Gathering (Malachi Smith)
The Highwayman, Pink Carnations and The Re-Allocated Coal
Scuttle (Revie)
The Mother Lode (Andrew Sparke)
Vital Nonsense (Andrew Sparke)
Walking The Edge (Various)
We May Win We May Lose (Jim Ryan)
Who'd Of Thought It (Lee Benson)
Wicked Virtue (Andrew Sparke)
Wild Verse (Andrew Sparke)
Word Bombs (Eddie Morton)